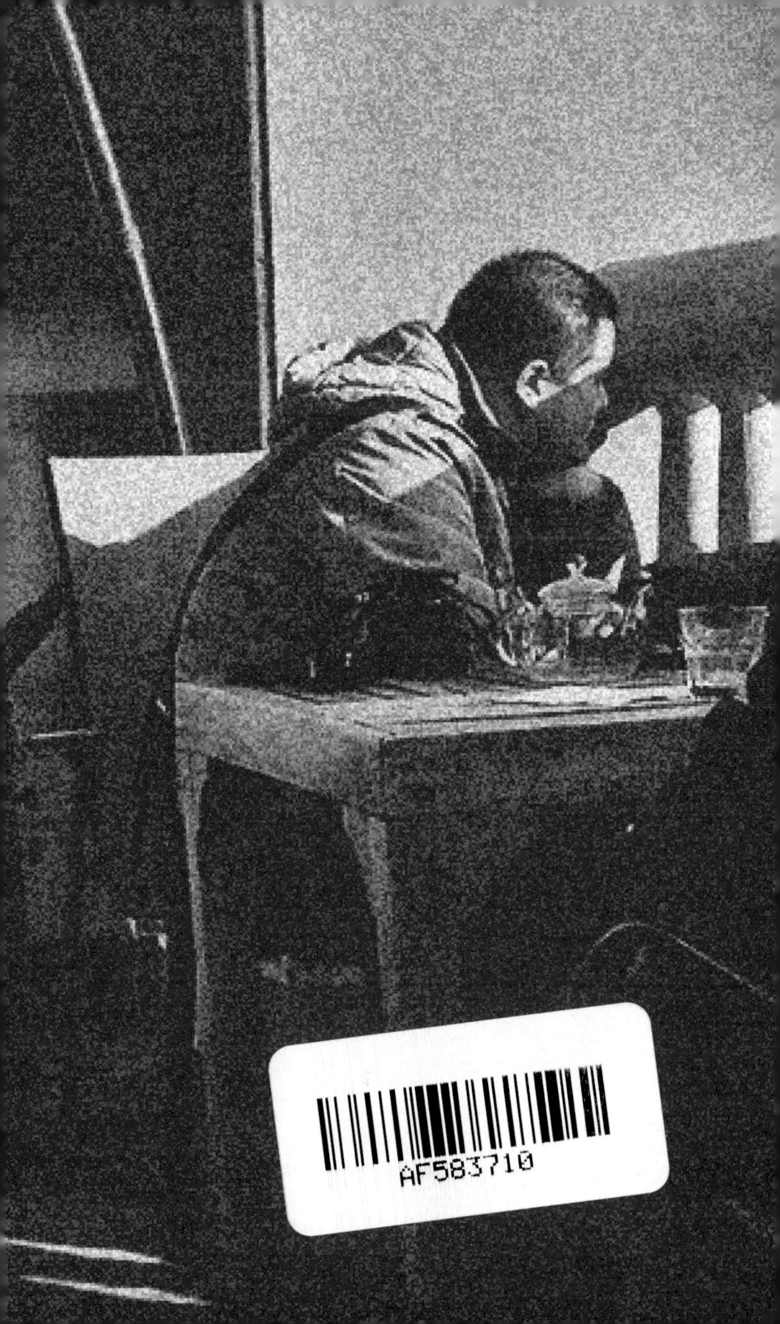

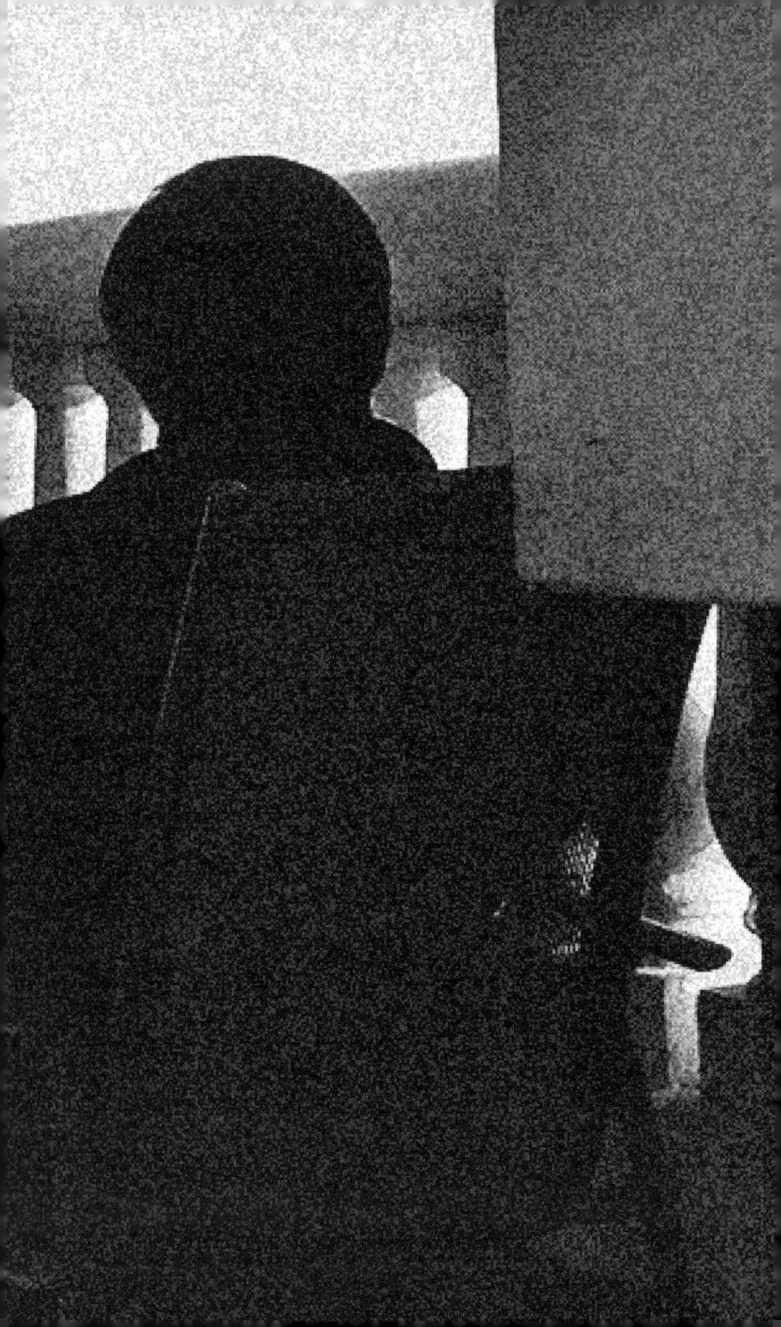

Ai Weiwei

On Censorship

AI WEIWEI

ON CENSORSHIP

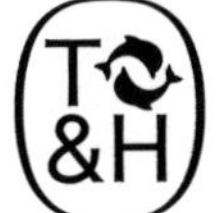

First published in the United Kingdom in 2026
by Thames & Hudson Ltd, 6–24 Britannia Street,
London WC1X 9JD

First published in the United States of America in
2026 by Thames & Hudson Inc., 500 Fifth Avenue,
New York, New York 10110

EU Authorized Representative: Interart S.A.R.L.
19 rue Charles Auray, 93500 Pantin, Paris, France
productsafety@thameshudson.co.uk
interart.fr

A CIP catalogue record for this book is available from
the British Library

Library of Congress Control Number 2025936048

ISBN 978-0-500-03082-0
01

Printed and bound in Italy by L.E.G.O. Spa

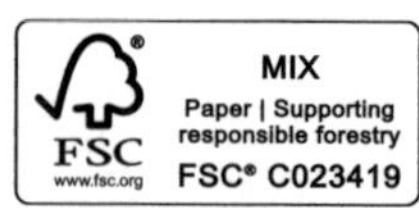

Contents

On Censorship

As a thinker and an artist, since 2009 I have found myself in irreconcilable conflict with the dominant ideologies of Chinese society – or, more precisely, with the official narrative propagated by the state. I have consistently raised questions about human value and rights, engaging in debates that inevitably touch on issues of social justice, fairness, the legitimacy of power and the execution of judicial justice, and I have put forward reflections on aesthetics, ethics and philosophy. While these thoughts may seem rough or incomplete, they are precisely the kinds of issues that those in power refuse to acknowledge, let alone discuss. The most effective method of dealing with such voices has been deletion and suppression – erasing them from public consciousness. The more thorough approach is to make the people behind these voices disappear altogether, or to push them beyond the borders of the state. I have experienced all of this first-hand.

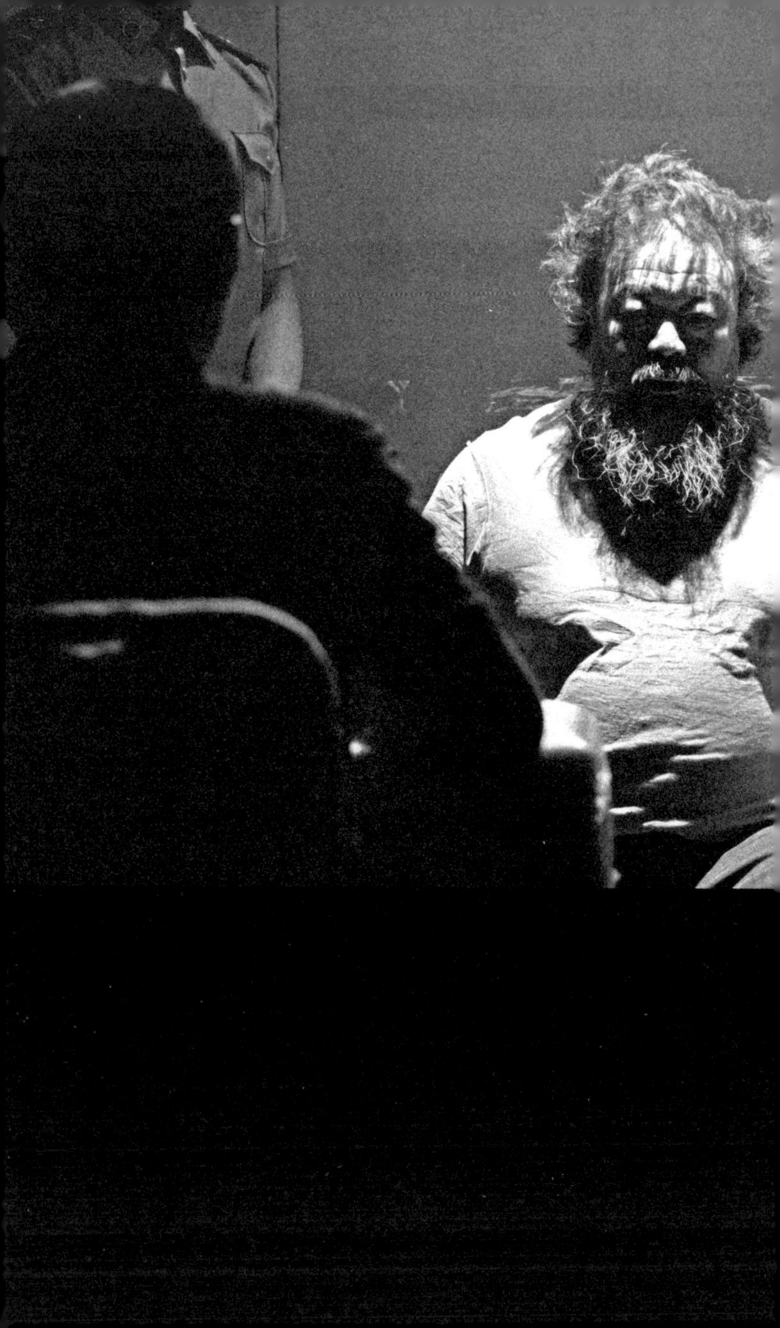

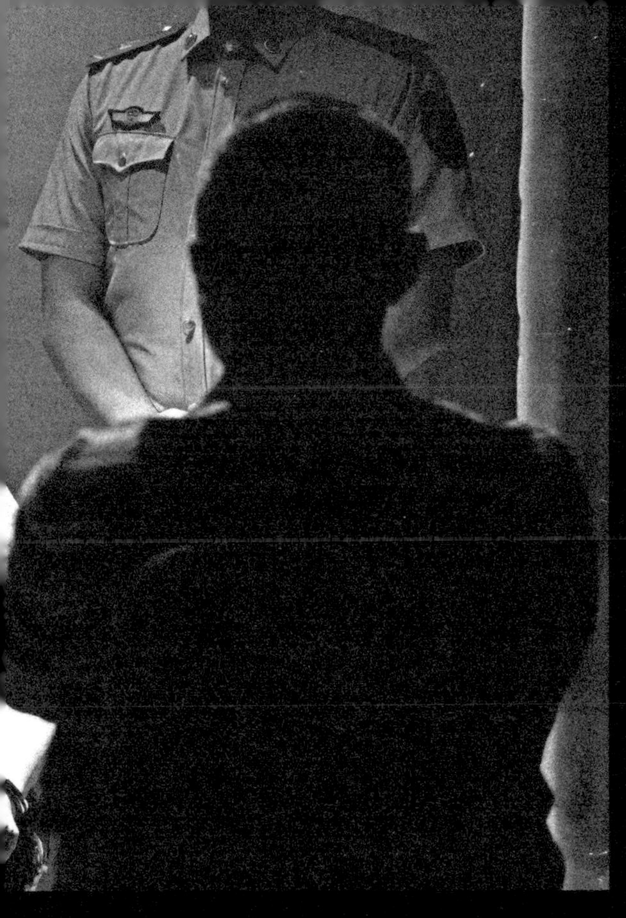

Still from *Dumbass*, music video, 2013. A re-enactment of Ai Weiwei's interrogation during his secret detention in 2011

What is Censorship?

Censorship usually refers to the actions of institutions with power or the dominant consciousness of society, encompassing religion and cultural value systems, to suppress non-mainstream ideologies, voices or expressions. This suppression may take the form of forceful, physical or mental prohibitions.

Censorship is often misunderstood, being typically associated with countries defined as autocratic and authoritarian. Without question, such systems thrive on strict ideological control and the suppression of dissenting voices. But this understanding overlooks other forms of suppression – and even inadvertently supports another perspective: that in societies considered relatively civilized or liberalized, and in those with democratic structures, censorship is either non-existent or extremely rare. This belief creates an impression of a stark contrast, akin to the difference between night and day – people forget that even on sunny days, shadows are inevitable. In reality, censorship exists everywhere. Wherever authority is present – be it political, economic or cultural – censorship is omnipresent. It seeps into every social being's existence, manifesting in different ways. By 'social beings', I refer to people whose actions are intertwined with the structures of society and whose potential for self-expression is shaped and constrained within these frameworks.

In ostensibly democratic societies – the democracies championed by the West, though whether they truly embody democratic principles or the ideals of the so-called free world is a matter for debate – thought and speech are subject to censorship through political, economic, media and social mechanisms. In many cases, this form of censorship is more covert, more deceptive and more corrosive. At its core, any form of censorship targets the dominant ideologies present within political and social structures. The essence of censorship is the control of thought – it is the exercise of power over intellectual space, involving the suppression and elimination of dissent. It can be described as both an indispensable tool of mental enslavement and a fundamental source of political corruption.

Distorted information or outright lies are inevitable tools of the censor. Freedom of speech and freedom of expression are the natural enemies of any censorship system.

The motives behind censorship have been embedded in human history since ancient times. One of the most significant functions of a country, political group or society can be expressed through a saying in circulation since the Shang period in China: 'the great affairs of the state are worship and military bases' (国之大事, 祀与戍). Worship involves paying homage to ancestors or spirits, serving to protect an established system and maintain control over discourse. This represents a nation's primary internal function. Meanwhile, military bases and defence ensure the state's survival and its capacity to wage war against external adversaries. Together, these two elements encapsulate the essential meanings of a country.

The worship of ancestors or spiritual powers that transcend human understanding is often blind and ritualistic, typically involving sacrifice – such as the burial of the living alongside the dead – to honour and sustain the power structure. Brutal as it may seem, it has proven historically effective, for the most precious thing in human life is life itself. In contemporary society, worship, once spiritual submission, has evolved into thought control, while 'military bases' take the form of military aggression. Widespread propaganda, brainwashing and media manipulation can be seen as contemporary forms of 'worship', while 'military bases' manifest in acts of invasion, war and genocide, all aimed at eliminating the physical presence or territorial identity of the perceived other. More often than not, these two mechanisms work in tandem.

Censorship is both brutal and effective. Its efficacy ensures the survival of existing political and economic systems; its brutality lies in the fact that, without censorship, the system would collapse and disintegrate, and thus censorship has never needed justification or mercy. It operates without apology or explanation. Whether it targets a country's president, a war effort, board members, professors in academia or anyone capable of transmitting information – such as artists, musicians and actors – censorship

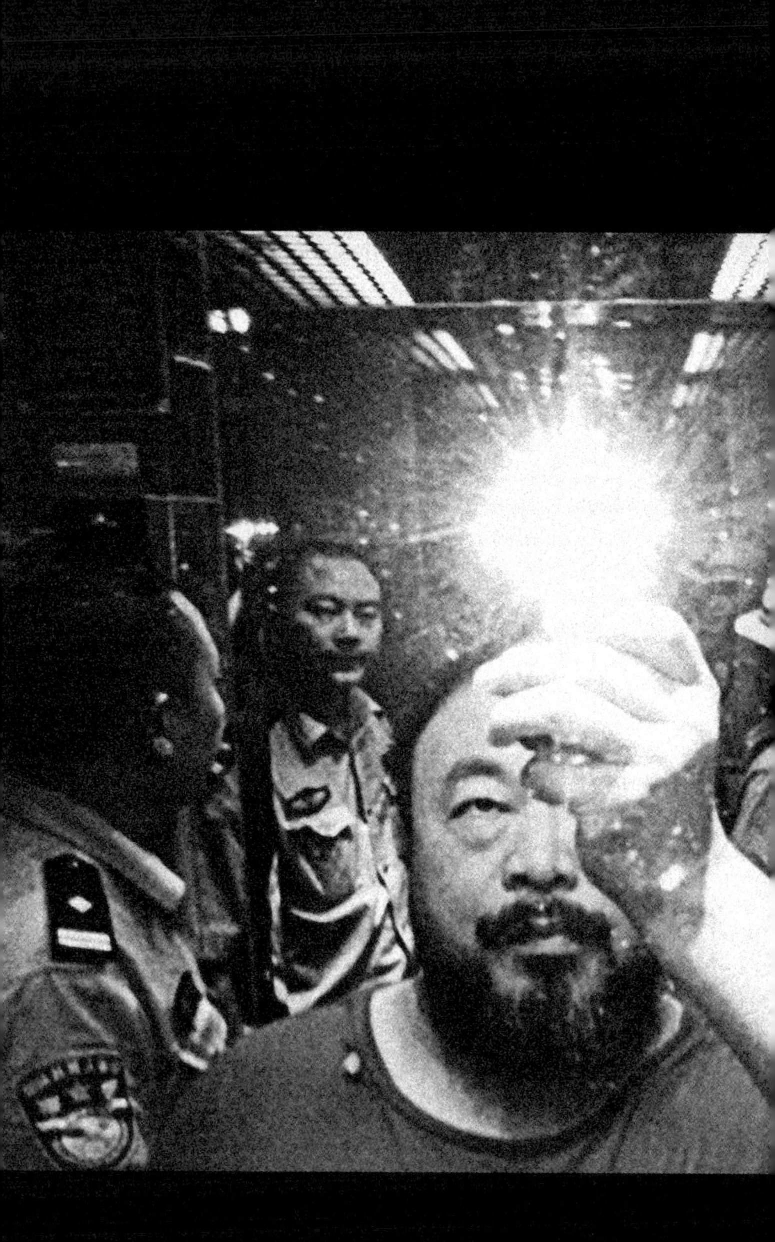

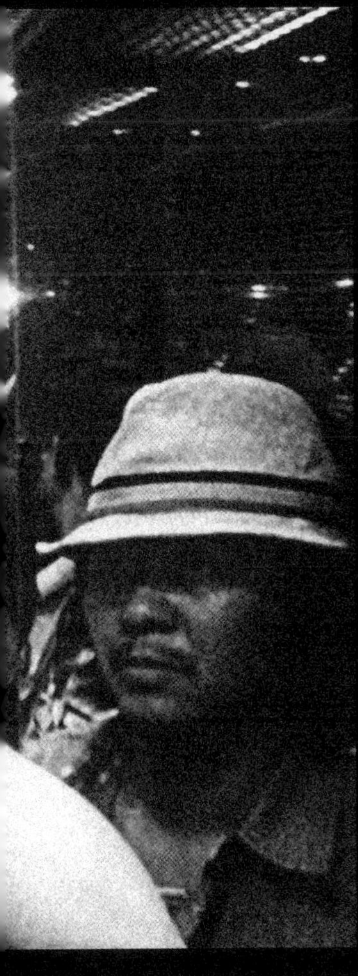

Illumination, 2009. A selfie taken in the elevator, while being taken away by policemen in Sichuan

demands sacrifices. These sacrifices are deemed necessary because, without them, society might follow the example of dissenters, which is seen as a terrifying possibility.

Censorship primarily relies on the power of intimidation. It targets those who dare to speak out first – individuals with clear attitudes, ethics, judgment and critical perspectives – by sanctioning them. This initial sanction sends a message: resistance is futile. It creates an environment in which most people feel powerless to resist or defend themselves, ensuring compliance through fear.

Censorship in China

The essence of censorship lies in the belief that certain thoughts or expressions – whether cultural, artistic or ideological – pose a threat to the mainstream value system and the legitimacy of power structures. Consequently, censorship, alongside war and military manoeuvres, becomes a key strategy for maintaining power. Mao Zedong famously noted that communists rely on military means to seize power and on the 'pen' to maintain it, with the latter symbolizing a regime's value system, ideology and propaganda. This concept, however, is not exclusive to twentieth-century Chinese revolutionary thought.

In China, censorship operates around the clock, infiltrating every channel of communication. It impacts all forms of personal expression related to the public, whether communicated through publications, art exhibitions or social networks. For over seventy years, censorship policies have been a core function of the regime and a widely accepted aspect of society.

In 2009, my name vanished from the public sphere. Within a month, my name and works were removed from two exhibitions and no art exhibitions thereafter mentioned my name or anything related to me.

When these events are viewed as part of a larger picture, the severity of the issue becomes clear. This strict censorship of information and expression not only affects individuals but also impacts the broader community of artists and society as a whole. For obvious reasons, art groups and institutions widely practice self-censorship to ensure their survival and protect their interests.

For instance, the director at the UCCA Center for Contemporary Art in Beijing revealed that they had received 'threats from above', leading to my exclusion from an exhibition. In China, the Party's censorship policies may not always directly target individuals but instead exert influence through your organization, landlord, relatives or colleagues. Even if you are independent, the system can impose a menacing influence on your environment, affecting everyone around you.

Intimidation is an effective tool by which to threaten the public. It not only successfully erases independent thought from the public domain and silences those who dare to express dissenting ideas, but also indoctrinates anyone hoping to remain part of society. To ensure economic security and personal safety, individuals are compelled to adhere to behavioural norms – asking no questions, refraining from judgment and avoiding attempts to discern right from wrong.

Censorship acts as an absolute authority over creativity, paralysing societal thought and stripping people of the courage to make judgments or take social responsibility.

Unlike most other parts of the world, China's internet operates as a closed local area network (LAN). Even this limited flow of information causes intense anxiety for the authorities. Internet censorship, which contradicts the very essence of the internet, has led to the arrest and imprisonment of many who fight for freedom of speech. While self-censorship remains widespread, the demand for freedom grows at an equally rapid pace. This paradox represents the dual challenges we face in our lives today.

Censorship in Western Societies

From a contemporary perspective, let's consider the United States or other western societies as examples. Censorship in these contexts does not operate solely through direct assertions, or power dictating what is right or wrong, good or bad, worth promoting or forbidding. Instead, it functions as part of a broader competitive capitalist system. This system uses wealth, safety and comfort as the core values upon which to construct the foundation of education and public discourse. Naturally, this is intertwined with traditional religious backgrounds – whether Christian, Muslim or other faiths – that point to a higher, invincible authority. For believers, this spiritual support underpins and sustains the prevailing power structures.

In modern, 'civilized' societies, the simple divinity of religion has been replaced by a sense of individual existence and material desire, often labelled as personal freedom and wealth. As for individual creativity and expression – they are, in most cases, forgotten. Such societies are dominated by the ideologies of so-called freedom and democracy, which themselves create fertile ground for a more covert form of censorship. This form of censorship subtly communicates that certain thoughts, speech or expressions are forbidden, not only because they diverge from societal values but because they pose a threat to individual existence. This threat undermines access to critical social structures such as family, friendships and employment.

A clear example of this lies in how, even under seemingly objective social judgments, those attempting to express truths are often labelled with politicized terms. These labels can crush individuals beneath the weight of society's dominant value system. The most effective tool of suppression is stripping people of their ability to survive and thrive, and their space for existence.

Specifically, when opposition to war or criticism of warring groups emerges, even the mildest and least confrontational critiques or simple statements of fact are often attributed with some form of anti-social characteristic – for example, criticism of Israeli forces' actions in Palestine, at universities such as Columbia University, being labelled anti-Semitic – erased from the media, and in some cases, targeted with incarceration and deportation. This is enough to destroy the social systems upon which an individual depends.

This phenomenon is far from isolated; it reflects a pervasive reality within ostensibly free and democratic societies. For artists, performances, publications and exhibitions are frequently cancelled, and the names of critics are sometimes entirely erased from media platforms.

Such actions compel people to ask: who wields this god-like power to shield obvious darkness and obscure the light of justice, preventing it from approaching fundamental truths and social fairness?

Self-Censorship

In the western world, censorship alone cannot achieve its goals; it relies heavily on self-censorship. This occurs when individuals, recognizing that their thoughts, expression or expressed attitudes – whether through language or artistic means – might provoke resistance or displeasure from those in power, adjust their behaviour to avoid conflict. In such circumstances, self-censorship emerges as a survival mechanism.

Censorship and self-censorship work hand-in-hand within society, ensuring that independent thought and creativity succumb to authority.

Self-censorship, often tied to the existential threat of survival, arises from a vague yet ingrained awareness of danger, requiring no direct orders from those in power. As the Chinese proverb 'kill the chicken to scare the monkey' suggests, punishing a single violator serves as a warning to the wider public. This tactic stokes fear and can influence not only individuals but entire generations.

For artists and writers, true thinking or expression must provoke observation, scrutiny or a sense of urgency about humanity's existence and its relationship with the surrounding world. If it fails to do so, it becomes self-censored, stripped of its meaning. When a work of thought or expression gains widespread public acceptance or adoration, it often signals a lack of depth or a fundamental misunderstanding of its purpose. This is why artists must maintain independence in their work; only through this can their thinking and expression retain their authenticity and impact. Without such independence, their existence becomes meaningless, reduced to mere conformity by popular acceptance.

For example, filmmaker friends of mine have shared instances in which their scripts, narrative structures, character dialogues and even use of specific terms have had to undergo rigorous scrutiny by various departments, including religious, military, cultural and propaganda authorities. Scripts have sometimes required hundreds of revisions, each accompanied by a system of rewards and penalties. The filmmakers were told that this process was the only way to secure approval, without which no one would invest in the project and, regardless of the actors involved, the finished film would neither reach the market nor generate box-office success.

In this stifling environment, directors and producers are like individuals caught in a relentless storm, unable to avoid being drenched. Self-censorship, then, becomes akin to trying to open an umbrella in the downpour. No matter how heavy the rain, the merest effort to shield oneself offers a chance to breathe and persist. This encapsulates the essence of self-censorship: a system of rewards and punishments designed to suppress or encourage certain aspects of human potential and expression. The process is comparable to training animals in a circus. Lions or monkeys are taught to perform specific gestures through repetitive methods of conditioning. Only through such training can these animals execute their movements flawlessly.

The Impacts of Censorship: The Legacy of Silence

The operation of censorship through intimidation and sanction is evident in the history of the Chinese Communist Party, which has seen more than fifty political movements over the decades. In every one, the first to be sanctioned were always those who refused to conform or collaborate – those with independent thought or differing political ideologies. Whether such thought is correct or not, even if the views may be flawed, they clearly stem from differing perspectives or questioning of political leaders or ideologies. The severity and breadth of sanctions for these differing views resulted in prolonged periods of silence, as no one dared to speak out for a decade or so. Those who once did are no longer present. It is all too easy to suppress, erase, outlaw or disappear.

My father, a poet, lived through such a time. During the thirty most expressive years of his life, he was silenced, forbidden from voicing his thoughts. His defiance came at a tremendous cost – his life was marked by suffering and our family endured punishment alongside him. Our experience was but a small reflection of what countless families endured. This political phenomenon and its accompanying methods of control turned China into a barren desert of thought, a place where no intellectual growth could take root.

This desolation has distinct characteristics. Censorship as a political system can be overt and tangible, such as the existence of a propaganda department within the Chinese Communist Party. Yet it can also be covert and diffuse, as seen in western countries, where corporations, lobbyists and political groups exert control through education systems, economic mechanisms and societal frameworks. These forces infiltrate and constrain the natural spaces for human thought and expression. The power of censorship is often subtle and imperceptible, yet its impact is undeniable. Paradoxically, when someone insists that it does not exist, they have, in fact, already proven its existence; its hidden and deceptive nature only enhances its influence.

The Impacts of Censorship: Relatively 'Open' Societies

Whether in autocratic regimes like China or in other, relatively open societies, censorship systems can be strikingly effective. But what are their inherent flaws in relatively open societies? Fundamentally, censorship is the natural enemy of human thought and expression. Thinking – the core of what it means to be human – is the most basic of rights, and freedom of thought is inextricably linked to freedom of speech. Without the ability to speak freely, the concept of free thought becomes meaningless. When censorship systematically eliminates freedom of speech and expression, it simultaneously erodes freedom of thought. This distorts humanity's intellectual and social systems, reducing them to values that serve only specific agendas or social frameworks.

This distortion is not confined to authoritarian regimes; it is evident also in western nations with self-professed civilized politics and democratic systems. The effects are both absurd and self-destructive, diverging from the fundamental values of human existence and the most basic moral principles. In such environments, societies fracture, divisions deepen and hatred festers. These divisions create fertile ground for conflict, wars and large-scale social problems that jeopardize humanity's living conditions and the possibilities for future development.

All this occurs when power, including ideological power or self-proclaimed superior and elitist thinking, replaces considerations of humanity's core survival needs. Such thinking, marked by absolutist and purifying tendencies reminiscent of Nazi ideology, undermines human values. Believing itself to act on behalf of nations or human civilization, this kind of censorship rejects differing viewpoints and labels them as backward, idiotic, uncivilized or conservative. These rejections are enforced through absolute and coercive measures. Such absolutism profoundly damages human thought as a living system, which thrives on diversity, differences, controversies and contradictions.

It is within such complex and inexplicable chaos that human thinking finds its vitality and the essential conditions for survival. Without such diversity, society inevitably moves towards the collapse of its intellectual ecosystem. When one mode of thought seeks to dominate others with claims of absolute progressiveness or advancement, society paradoxically veers into anti-human territory.

What does Censorship Aim For?

A primary aim of censorship is to normalize itself, to present itself as natural and essential. It frames its existence as necessary, its rights as justified and its sanctions as reasonable. By establishing these attributes, censorship embeds itself into society as an unquestioned rationale. This normalization is the most insidious aspect of censorship – it undermines individual consciousness, goodwill and tolerance. It stifles the critical processes of understanding, self-doubt and self-challenge, which are vital functions of thought. A society that pursues uniformity of stance, conformity of opinion and political correctness, in which all functions of independent thought are excluded, will inevitably become weak, absurd and corrupt – a society devoid of reason.

Censorship relies on the perceived legitimacy of power, while stripping away the legitimacy of human dignity and nature. This phenomenon is not unique to authoritarian regimes; it is also prevalent in western societies, where its existence is undeniable.

The legitimacy of power has been used to replace and override the legitimacy of humanity's most basic dignity and fundamental rights. This substitution and dominance is widespread in so-called democratic societies in the West, and equally beyond dispute.

Cloaked in the guise of a natural force, censorship ensures widespread compliance among the majority of people in most circumstances. This mass ideology holds a firm grip on society, influencing every decision and choice individuals make, from grand political judgments to the smallest personal decisions. In this distorted environment, public consciousness is shaped not by genuine individual choices but by the confines of a politically correct framework – a sphere of artificial conformity that is irresistible.

Generally speaking, censorship fosters popular conformity and functions as a dominant and controlling field of mainstream consciousness. It is so powerful that it dictates movements, behaviours and actions, and shapes the very spheres in which thought and expression can occur. Such spheres, particularly in today's mainstream media, are often catastrophic. We see the pervasive distortion of truth, driven by the need to safeguard the profits of major corporations and capital, while those in power reject the most basic facts.

The data on climate change, for example, has been consistently suppressed by governments and profit-driven interest groups. Or as another example, take my investigation into the deaths of schoolchildren during the Sichuan earthquake in 2008.

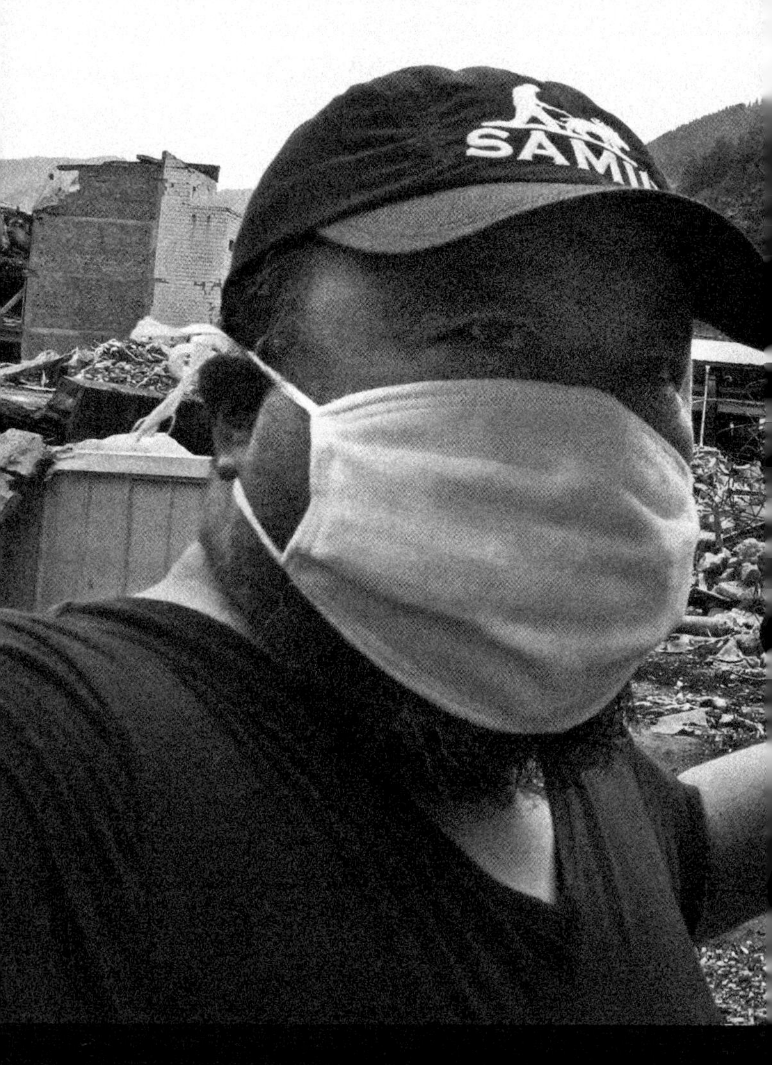

Ai Weiwei conducting a Citizens'
Investigation in Sichuan, 2008

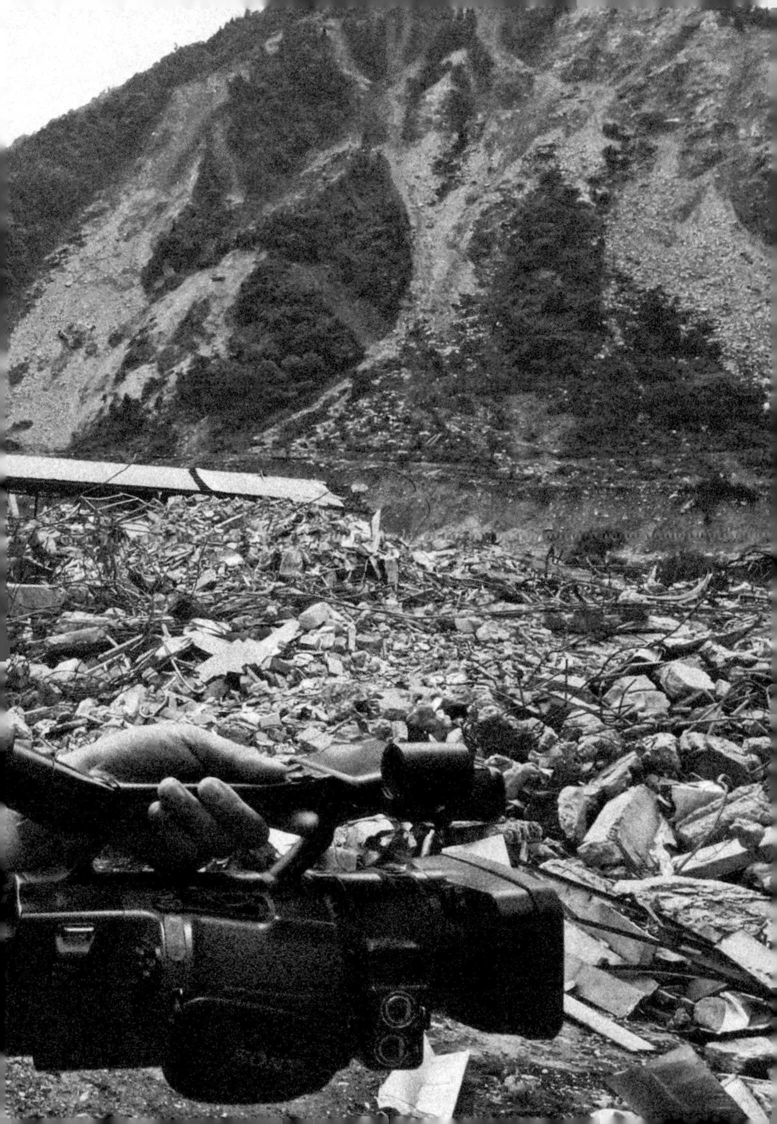

I was not engaged in a political struggle. I was simply advocating for respect for life and the refusal to forget by demanding transparency of information. It was an extremely measured stance; I believe that only when concrete numbers emerge can the public begin to reflect on such abnormal events or phenomena.

Or consider the Israel–Gaza conflict: how many bombs have been used? How many journalists have been injured or killed? These numbers often surpass anything we can imagine. Yet providing false figures is a common governmental tactic. A flood of distorted information is pushed onto public platforms, making it difficult for people to access accurate facts. Eventually, this leads many to abandon the pursuit of truth altogether, as objective facts are drowned out – or even obliterated – by manipulation and deception. This damages independent and critical thinking, eroding the basic honesty and reliability of modern civilization.

Censorship effectively eliminates public and societal participation. It suppresses the public's ability to question fundamental issues of honesty, of what has happened and how. This power is both invisible and omnipresent. It strips innocence from the young and kindness from the elderly. It discourages people from valuing justice, fostering selfishness instead. Values such as effort, responsibility and the preservation of life's dignity are replaced by materialism, fleeting pleasure and shallow entertainment.

Card Games

Each player in a game has their own hand of cards, known only to themselves. The remaining cards and those already revealed are public information, shared openly and fairly. The cards yet to be disclosed remain unknown and ultimately determine the winner and loser.

Players only agree to participate in the game if they trust that the undisclosed cards will remain unchanged until they are revealed. Whether in culture or politics, democracy or authoritarianism, the dealer holds an absolute advantage if they know the value of the undisclosed cards first. This advantage stems from technological and policy dominance, supported by special rules and laws. Unfair conditions are often justified by opacity, frequently under the pretext of enhanced security to combat the spectre of terrorism. But why do we allow ourselves to play such an unfair game?

Society has largely accepted the notion that data obtained through surveillance constitutes facts and truth. Yet in most cases, the results of surveillance are themselves shaped by selective material, omitted or retained content, digital reconstruction and the context in which the data is interpreted. These results are not real-time truths but analysed, interpreted and selectively disseminated realities.

Much like photography, information gathered through surveillance raises questions: is it drawn from reality itself or merely a distorted description of it? Does the context of the information align with the image it presents? What was the original intent of the recording? Public reactions can, in fact, be manipulated through the presentation of a curated reality.

The Deceived Audience

When a magician performs on stage, everything appears flawless. A rabbit emerges from a hat; the card you selected is drawn from the deck. The miracle unfolds before your eyes.

In 2011, I was secretly detained for eighty-one days. My interrogators fabricated accusations, attempting to shake my commitment to truth and justice or tarnish my reputation. I found them absurd – and so did those interrogating me. They knew the accusations were made up and seemed almost amused by them. Looking into their eyes, I asked, 'You use these kinds of charges – economic crimes, debauchery – do you really think the younger generation outside will believe them?' After a brief pause, one of them confidently replied, 'Weiwei, ninety-nine per cent of them will.' This response revealed something essential: in these matters, power is not concerned with good or bad, right or wrong. Those in power operate on the fundamental belief that the understanding of the masses can be manipulated according to what is most effective.

When governments or institutions disseminate false information, they shield themselves from truthful judgment – the kind of truth no authority can withstand. That captivated audience – the ninety-nine per cent – will always exist, and they are the magician's target.

Surveillance

Surveillance has existed since the dawn of human intelligence, or more precisely, since humanity became aware of its independent, yet interdependent, coexistence. With this awareness arose the inherent desire to watch and to be watched. Surveillance has long since become an integral part of modern life, encompassing everything from espionage and the monitoring of high-level political figures to the minutiae of everyday personal activities. It is all-encompassing and omnipresent. As technology advances rapidly, surveillance is increasingly accepted as a routine aspect of society.

Reality itself has shifted from being purely a physical phenomenon to a more abstract, mysterious narrative shaped by interpretations of truth and fact. Power, driven by scientific, economic and military motives, propels technological development, with observation and data collection serving as technology's most fundamental and valuable efforts. Everyone is inevitably, inescapably woven into the fabric of this network. The existence and mechanisms of surveillance remain both familiar and alien, requiring redefinition. Modern surveillance operates in a dual language of physical and virtual dimensions.

At its core, surveillance is used to identify and target subjects and assist in drawing conclusions about these individuals, groups or entire societies. It serves as a means of gathering intelligence and making value judgments about those deemed questionable or unknown.

Surveillance only wields power when individuals voluntarily participate; a magician's power comes from the audience inviting them to perform. It is exactly because people seek truth that surveillance works, but the truths they receive are provided by those with the power to surveil. The surveilled have

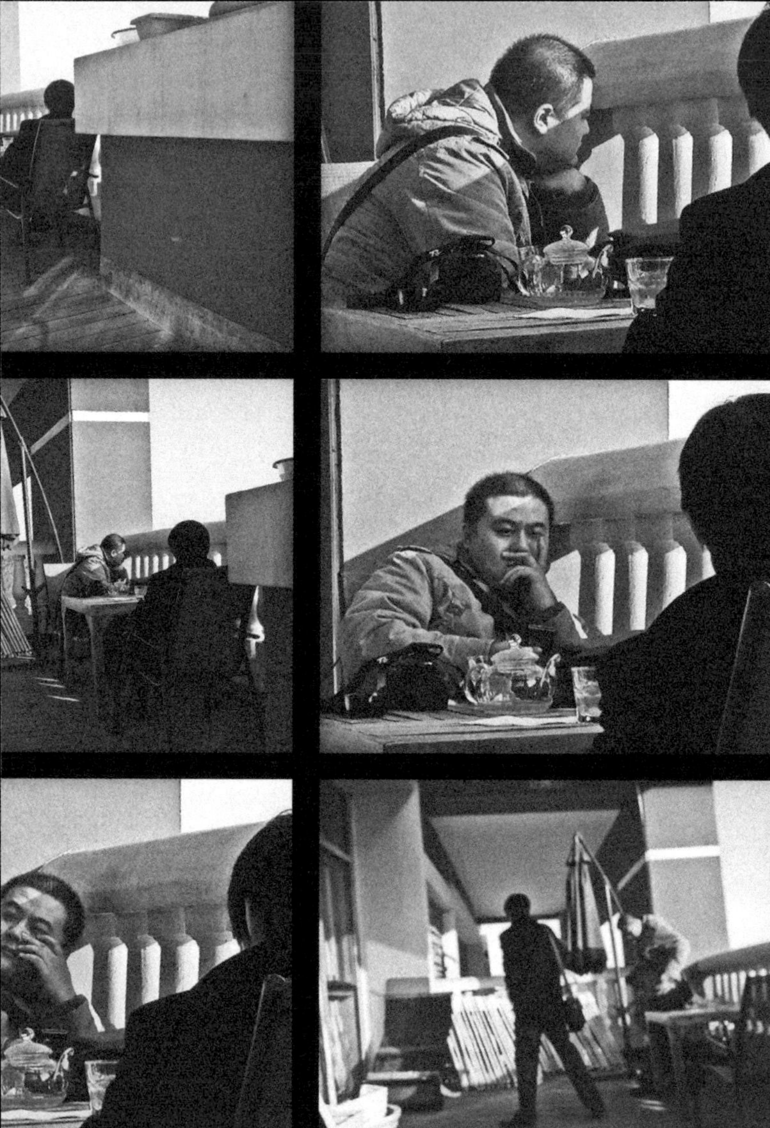

Undercover policemen surveilling Ai Weiwei, photographs by Ai Weiwei, 2012

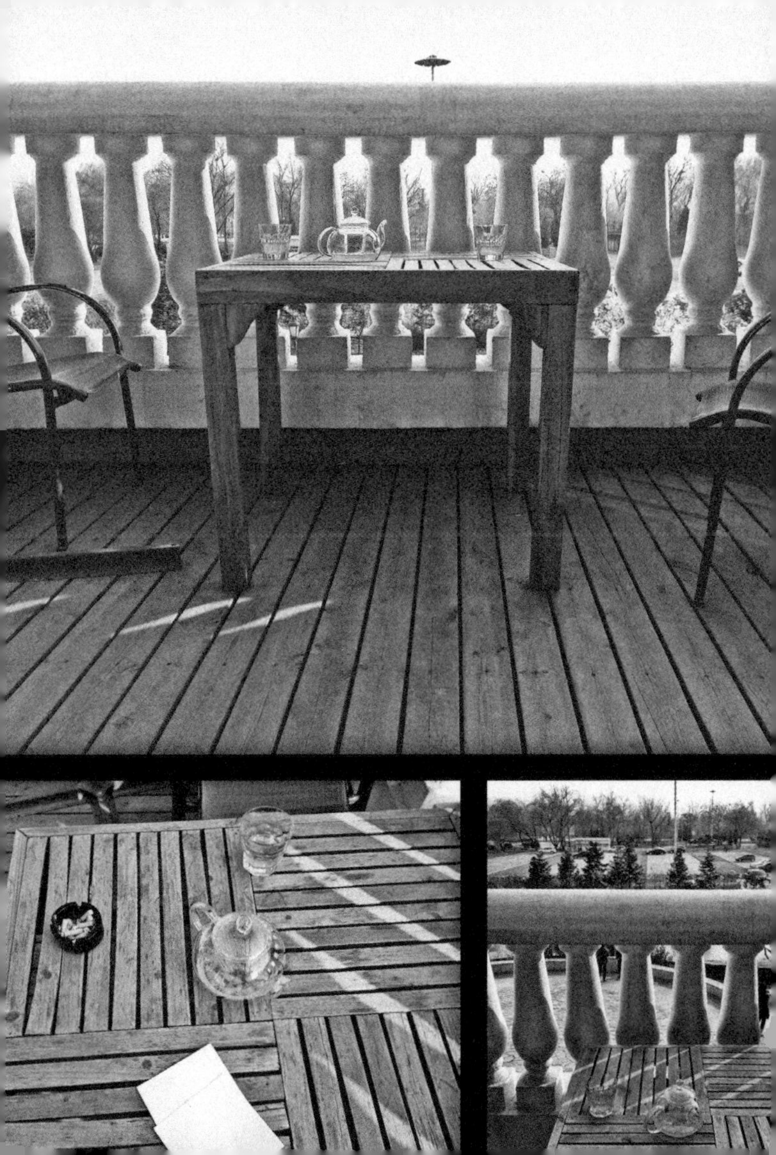

no choice but to accept altered truths. The audience wants to watch, to witness with their own eyes. They don't even need to be convinced; deceived yet enthralled, they applaud enthusiastically. This is a stark reflection of our society.

In any game, your willingness to play relies on a belief in fairness. If the game is merely an illusion, you've already lost. Why waste time playing a game you can never win?

Argos Panoptes

Surveillance is an ever-watchful eye. It brings to life Argos Panoptes, the one-hundred-eyed giant of Greek mythology. Argos Panoptes offers a new understanding of what runs parallel to truth and reality: the power of constant observation, when every action is monitored, recorded and capable of being replayed. Modern surveillance has changed the rules of the game, as those in power seek not only to know more about you, but to make you constantly aware that you are being watched. This serves two key purposes.

First, authorities can weaponize the data collected in the name of evidence or truth. By selectively disclosing distorted fragments of information, they are able to craft potent tools for attack. These fragments might include where you've been, who you associate with or what you've said or done in your most private moments.

In China, for example, police control CCTV footage but rarely present unedited images or videos, often citing technical glitches as the reason. In the United States, cases of police misconduct frequently go unresolved due to 'malfunctioning' surveillance cameras or missing surveillance footage. The partial truths they present obscure the full reality. Without access to the complete and unaltered information, the game is always one-sided. The public is left misled and exploited by the pretence of transparency.

When carrying out an arrest in the United States, police give the Miranda warning: 'You have the right to remain silent and refuse to answer questions. Anything you say can and will be used against you in court.' With surveillance, the right to not be

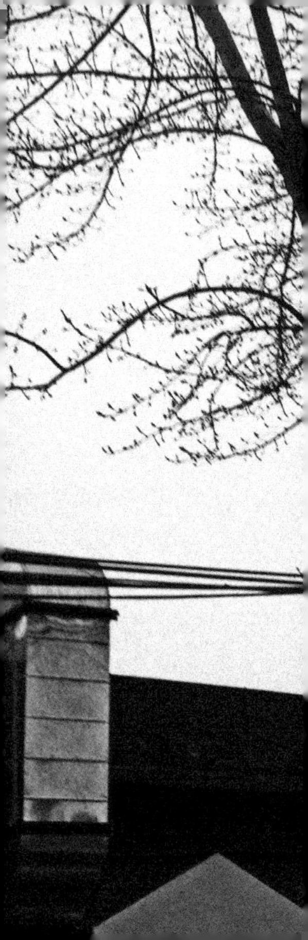

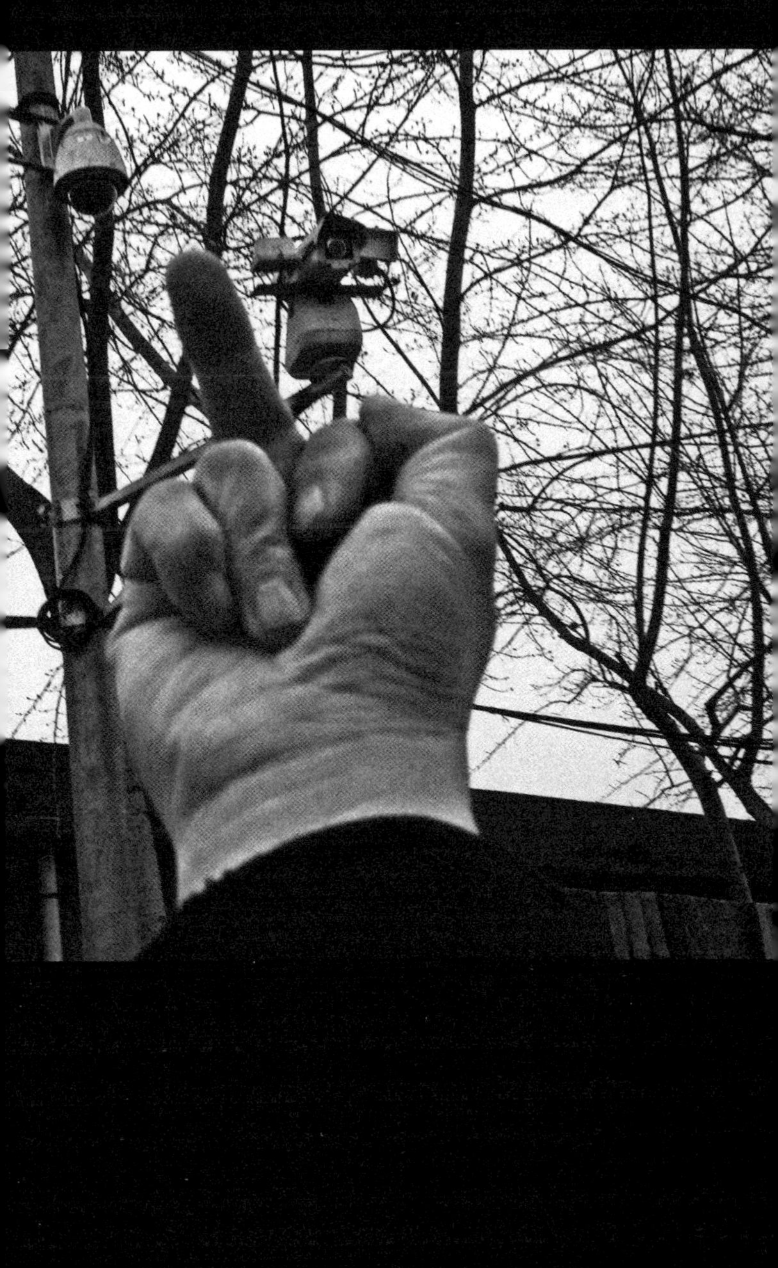

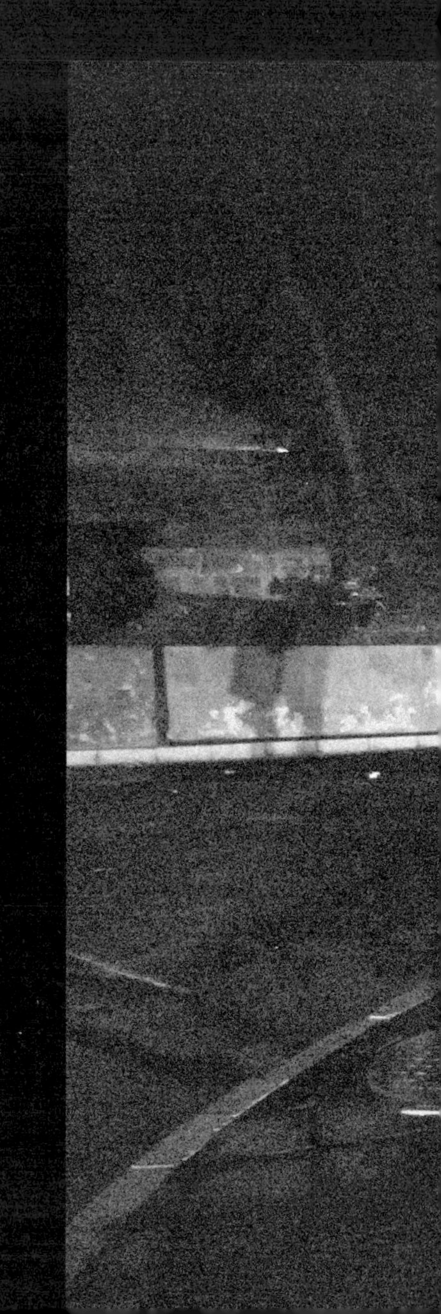

A surveillance vehicle outside Ai Weiwei's studio, Beijing, 2012

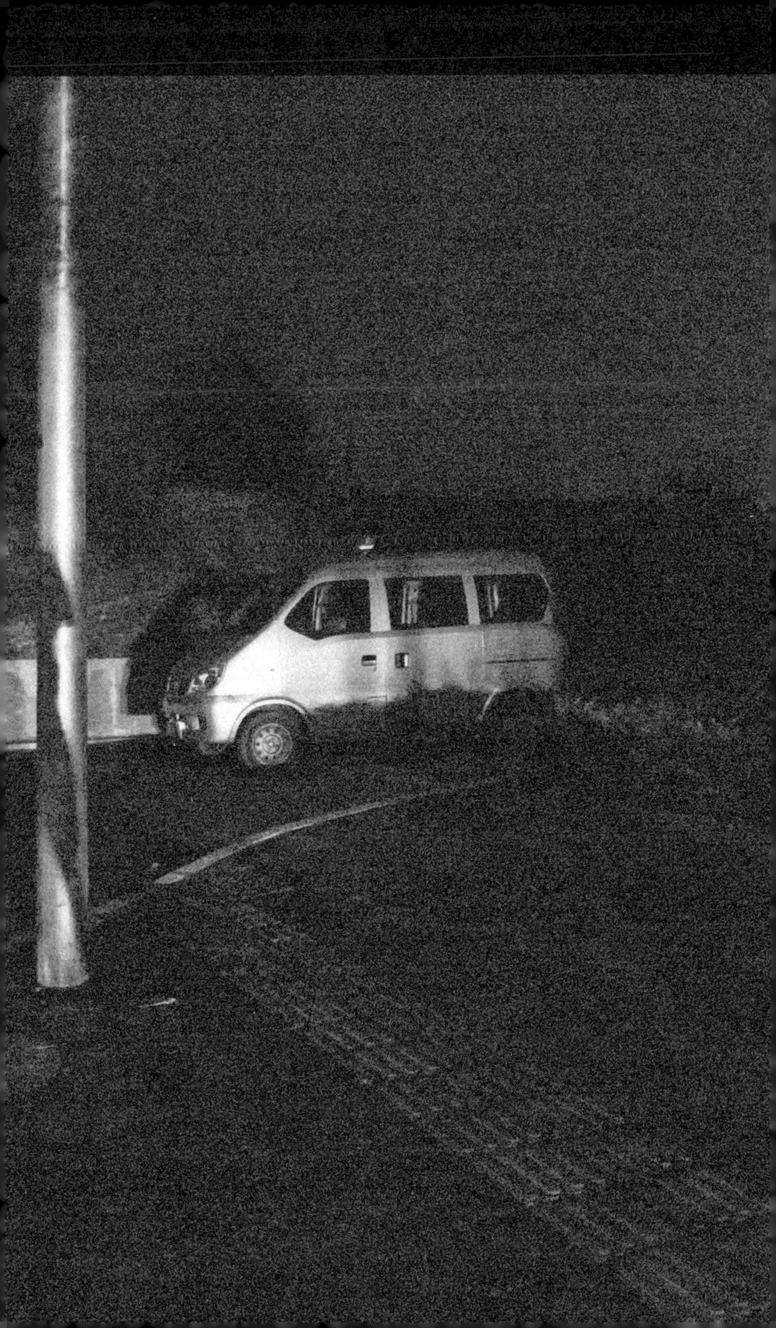

watched no longer exists. Everything collected can and will be used against you.

Second, damage can be inflicted merely by announcing the existence of recordings or evidence – without revealing them. The suggestion of surveillance often carries consequences far greater than the reality. The act of spying on someone's life without their awareness, or openly declaring the ability to do so, exerts a powerful psychological effect, altering behaviour. You may or may not be under surveillance, but you can never be sure; this uncertainty leads not only to self-censorship but to paranoia. It's like standing between two mirrors: you can see yourself, but who else might be watching?

Understanding the Unknown

The degree of exposure directly correlates with public curiosity – the more private the matter, the more significant and intriguing it becomes. Take, for instance, Michael Flynn, the retired United States Army lieutenant general who refused to testify in the investigation into Russian interference in the 2016

U.S. elections. What exactly does U.S. intelligence know? The public's focus is on whether something did or did not happen. The unknown compels us to seek answers, its vastness comparable to the universe itself.

Knowing too much can sometimes rob us of the joy of imagination and dreaming. When we first saw the image of a footprint on the moon, centuries of poetry and literary musings about the moon came to a halt. Nobody cared about lunar myths anymore. Paradoxically, the more we learn, the more we lose.

People believe that civilization is progressing towards enlightenment. Knowledge grants us self-awareness, shapes our understanding of human rights and provides clarity on equality and justice. But 'enlightenment' is an outdated measure. Where new technologies once promised greater equality and a utopian future, they have instead raised more problems than solutions. We are not born equal; we have instead become creatures guided by unknown forces that we do not understand. We live in a state of heightened uncertainty, increasingly sceptical of the information that surrounds us. Our judgment, our ability to discern fact from fiction, is under relentless pressure – a pressure that numbs the soul.

Suddenly, you find yourself standing helpless in a vast wilderness, lost. Your sense of trust disappears, as we now inhabit fragmented realities and conflicting truths. In our quest for clarity, we have become disoriented. Our dependence on virtual reality grows to the point where the tangible world loses its significance. While our traditional understanding of size, shape, texture, temperature, sound, lines and light remains, these elements also exist in virtual reality, fundamentally altering our perception of existence.

Today, individuals need no longer get lost. New technologies can guide us through even the most unfamiliar environments, tracking our steps, calculating calories burned and providing the temperature of any location worldwide. But these technologies are tools manipulated by people. We can see that big data is not objective reality; rather, it raises the stakes in the struggle for power, making it even harder to distinguish between what is true and what is not. These power structures can effortlessly trace people, examining records of text messages, emails and phone calls to determine who you've contacted; tracking your movements via GPS; even installing listening devices in your home or hotel room to eavesdrop on private conversations. They can construct a comprehensive, all-encompassing map.

In 2015, when I discovered hidden listening devices installed inside the power outlets of my studio, I was unsettled by the relentless efforts of those in power and the uneasy relationship this revealed between me and my homeland. Hearing a story about a snake is one thing; finding a snake writhing under your table is entirely different – especially when it's alive and you can't kill it. Later, the authorities went so far as to plead with me to return the surveillance device, fearing the exposure of their tools.

Individuals are inevitably thrown into confusion, because surveillance infiltrates every trace of our lives. These traces are the imprints we leave behind – the sum of every choice we make, our language, political views, education, traditions and social circles. They are the raw material for art, architecture, literature, poetry and music. These traces exist in every human activity, and beyond them, we leave

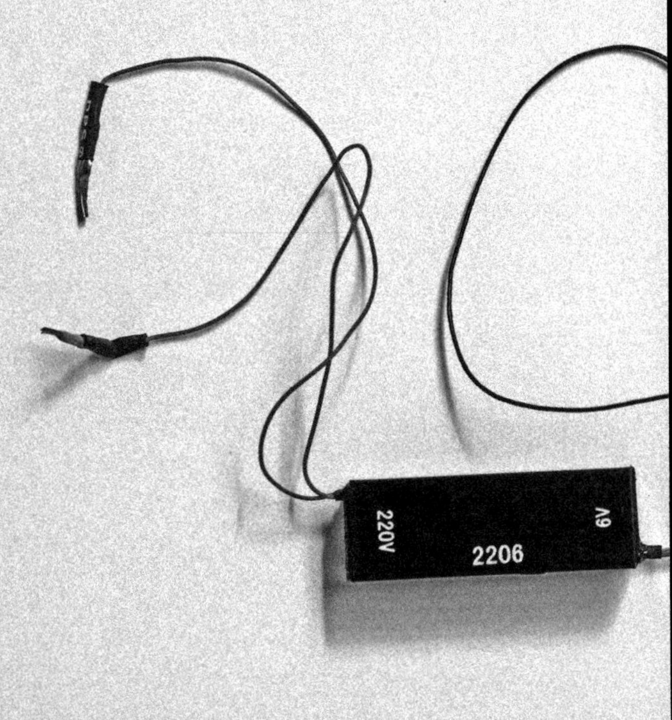

A detectaphone found in
Ai Weiwei's studio, Beijing, 2015

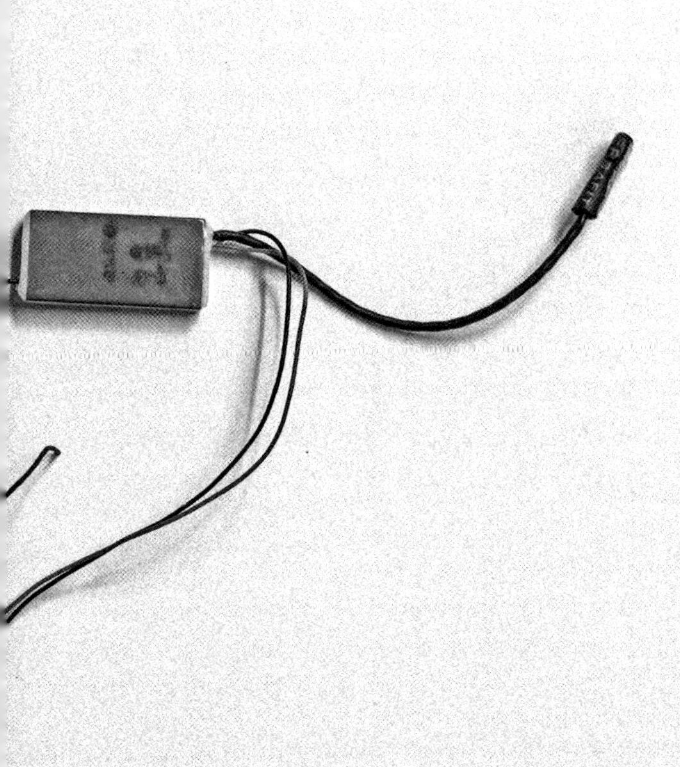

no legacy. Existence itself becomes an illusion. The things we hold dear are transformed into data, scrutinized by power without our consent. The phrase 'none of your business' loses all meaning.

Censorship and Privacy

What is privacy, and why is it so important? Discussing censorship inevitably leads to examining the origins of privacy – how it has been shaped, and how technological revolutions have transformed surveillance systems. These changes profoundly affect individuals, society and the values underpinning existence itself, marking a fundamental shift in human reality.

Under the influence of big data and new technologies, the capabilities of censorship and surveillance systems have undergone revolutionary changes. In the past, censorship was limited to monitoring writings, speech or visual exchanges, relying on the traces people left behind to identify and suppress dissent, with its efficacy depending on a cycle of punishment and reward. But with today's technological progress, censorship now encompasses the minutiae of human existence. It extends from genetic data to the smallest details of a person's life, including facial recognition, interactions with others, spoken words, consumption habits and every step taken. Social media activity – what individuals engage with, like, share or react to – has become instantly accessible for analysis, often beyond the individual's own awareness or control.

The scope, depth and reach of modern censorship are unparalleled in human history, surpassing even the most dystopian visions of science fiction. The extent of surveillance creates a surreal, almost magical scenario that defies comprehension. And it comes with devastating consequences: the collapse of foundational human values. The personal right to privacy is a defining characteristic of individual existence, but concepts such as personal rights, individual consciousness and the fundamental quality of personal privacy are now being systematically dismantled.

Personal privacy is the right of an individual to own and protect aspects of their life that they do not wish to disclose or share. It serves as the moral

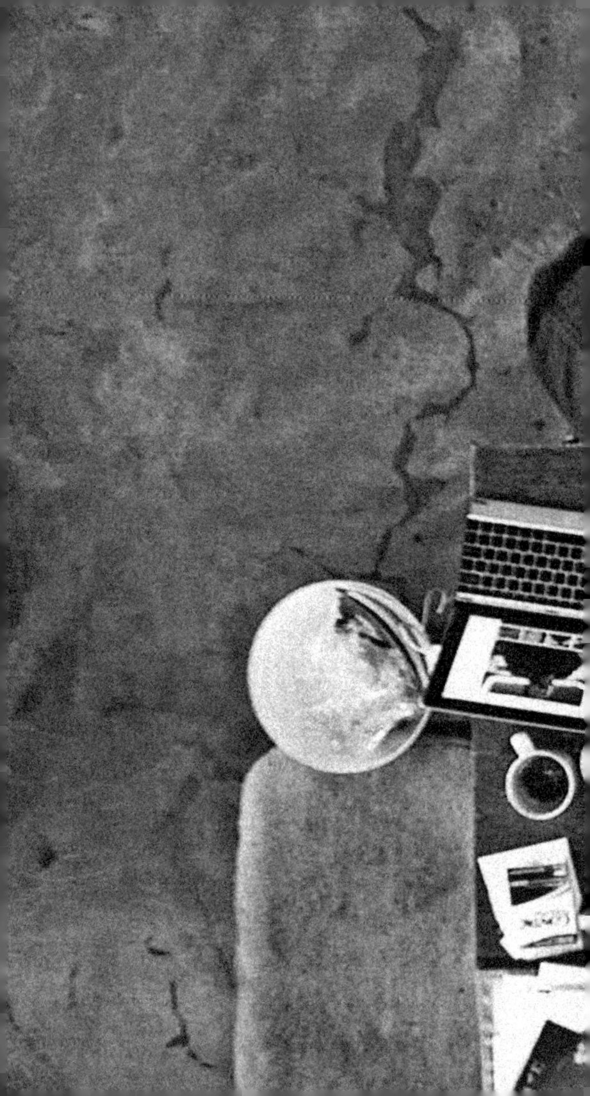

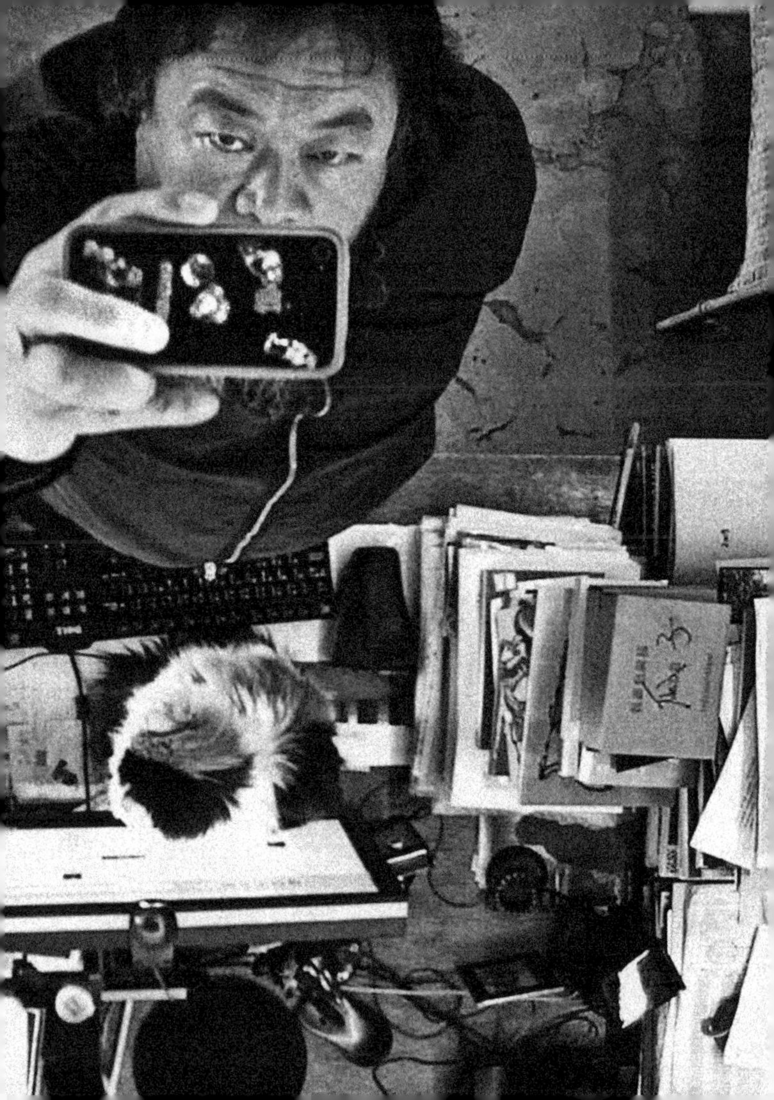

Image from WeiweiCam, Weiwei's online self-surveillance project, 2012. This was a 24-hour live broadcast of his own surveillance.

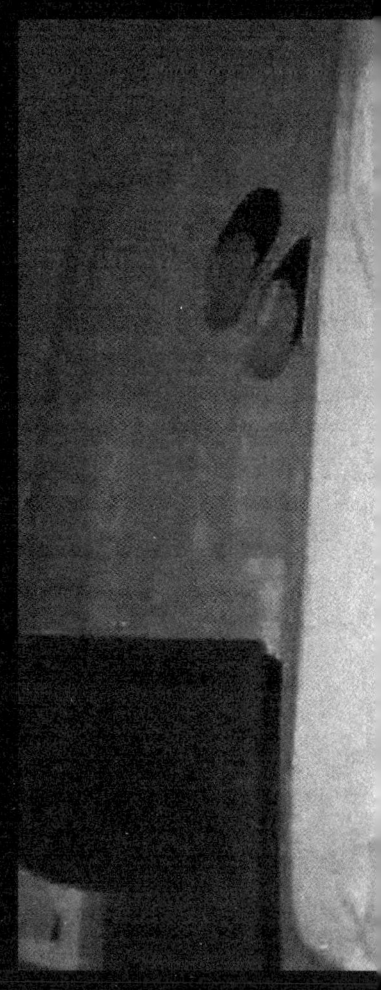

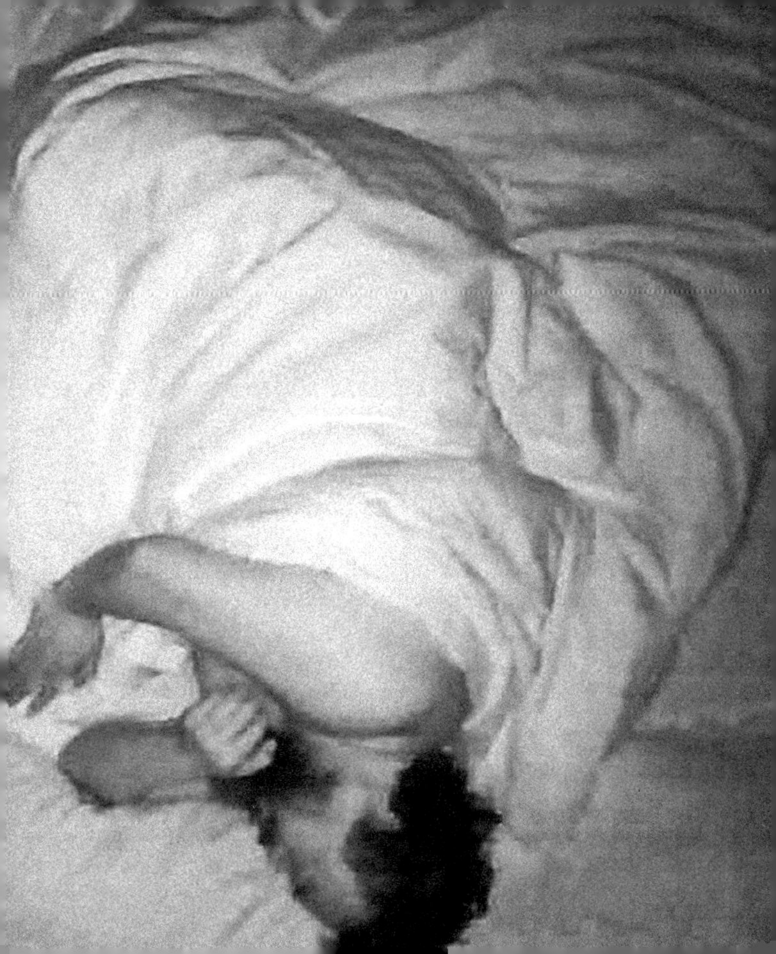

foundation for faith, profession, family, friendship and trust. Privacy ensures that certain aspects of a person's life remain unexposed and undisplayed, free from interference, questioning or scrutiny by public values, and exempt from examination or rejection based on political, ideological or religious differences. It encompasses the unknown or hidden aspects of one's life. Privacy safeguards the individual's ultimate right to own their inherent value and qualities – a right that fundamentally distinguishes one person from others or from the collective.

Under the control of technological power, authority can extend its reach into human interaction patterns, consumer information, health conditions and behavioural traces. Comprehensive, omnipresent and all-encompassing surveillance technologies have rendered traditional notions of personal privacy obsolete.

When personal privacy ceases to exist, the essential characteristics of individuality also vanish. In this scenario, information controllers – whether at the technological, political, economic or moral level – become objective forces within systems of technological manipulation, government authority, commercial power and ideological surveillance.

Surveillance, from its inception to full realization, signals to the surveilled that the power of censorship has been infinitely magnified. Effortless and precise, it holds the potential to eliminate any dissenting thoughts or behaviours. This warning surpasses humanity's understanding of self and personal space – or, more accurately, this space no longer exists. Under the control of technological analysis, life's unique information is reduced to indistinguishable sameness, flattened into irrelevance. As a result, people become slaves to a system that permeates every aspect of life: interpersonal relationships, existence, self-awareness, family dynamics, societal structure, production systems and social exchanges.

With the disappearance of individual privacy, the relationship between humans and the world has undergone an irreversible transformation. Humanity has simultaneously lost one of its most essential ethical and moral foundations – the trust and ecological coexistence between different beings – that is crucial for social survival. Trust and honesty have become irrelevant. The sense of individual existence now carries the potential for self-harm; it becomes the first aspect to be eliminated. Individuality and self-consciousness are inevitably viewed as defects and threats. The threat to the individual is difficult to detect, as the process of deterioration is latent yet omnipresent – like a terminal illness, pervasive and invisible.

This dystopian reality surpasses even the imagination of works like George Orwell's *1984*, which grapple with the concept of censorship. Big data undermines both the value of individual existence and the collective worth of humanity as a whole.

When an individual exists within the framework of comprehensive data collection and analysis, what one sees and becomes aware of, every action and interaction, takes place under its scrutiny and analysis, subject to constant surveillance and interpretation. Individuals are reduced to a transparent, jelly-like state within society – formless, uniform and stripped of distinction. This disappearance of individuality resembles ghosts inhabiting bodies, impossible to exorcise. In such a state, individuals cannot struggle or resist. The primal human drive to assert difference and autonomy has been dismantled by today's technological systems, driven by desires for control, creating a stark new reality.

This marks perhaps the most profound and complete de-individualization of humanity. A new societal attribute, a new kind of humanity emerges. It manifests in the superficiality of all values, in entertainment-driven distractions and in self-inflicted harm, as humanity's mutual trust and honesty gradually erode. Responsibility, duty and integrity disappear along with this; honesty loses its value, and concepts like sincerity, hypocrisy and deceit cease to hold any meaning.

Utilizing technological big data, power becomes stronger than ever before. Censorship is merely its precondition, by which it now wields disproportionately expanding control and an unprecedented monopoly over information and knowledge.

Censorship in the Age of AI

In 2025, the rapid development of artificial intelligence pushed a group of young Chinese entrepreneurs to the forefront with DeepSeek, which propelled its search technology into new territories. This triggered panic within the highly competitive AI landscape, sparking strategic shifts in western-dominated technology ecosystems and causing significant market disruptions. Once again, it forces us to reflect deeply on the rise of AI in the information age. At its core, AI represents a mythical level of information control, which is also the very foundation of any censorship system.

An interesting incident occurred when people tested this new AI tool by asking about me. The AI's response was blunt: 'Let's talk about something else.' This is precisely the problem. For decades, the Chinese regime has employed similar strategies – refusing to acknowledge the existence of certain topics, denying freedom of expression, enforcing censorship and systematically purging dissent. While loudly proclaiming slogans like 'A Shared Future for

Mankind' and 'One World, One Dream', the regime meticulously censors and suppresses the contradictions embedded in reality.

Censorship poses the same challenges to both Chinese and western technological development. In the pursuit of economic and political advantage, humanitarian values and human rights principles are crumbling. At the same time, China's relentless, self-aggrandizing ambition faces an insurmountable contradiction. Freedom of speech and expression is fundamental to human happiness and development. No matter how powerful China becomes, it cannot escape these ideological 'immune system' flaws. Suppressing dissent and purging heterodox thinking will only lead to catastrophic consequences for humanity when combined with new technologies. As we enter the AI era, human collective thought patterns, ideological structures and the very essence of individual existence and dignity are undeniably under threat.

Artificial intelligence struggles to function fairly, because its judgment, based solely on existing data, is inherently limited. As a result, its conclusions can be biased. For instance, ChatGPT misjudged a selfie I took with a leader of the Alternativ für Deutschland party, Alice Weidel, wrongly identifying it as a fabricated image. ChatGPT's rationale was based on the information that Ai Weiwei, known for advocating for human rights, supporting migrants and defending minority groups, would never pose for a selfie with such a figure, the chair of a right-wing populist, nationalist political party. This conclusion was drawn from pre-existing assumptions and social narratives about both me and the other individual. It was inaccurate. What this reveals is telling: ChatGPT, and AI more broadly, is not capable of delivering factual, objective judgments. Instead, it draws upon the prevailing biases, moral and ethical codes embedded in society, often leading to simplistic, even erroneous conclusions.

The growth of AI has been likened to the spread of a virus or a pandemic, with one crucial difference: it is irreversible. Big data reduces human thought and information to banal, homogenized content, processed unconsciously and indiscriminately through recycling, reorganizing and reapplying knowledge, akin to waste management. In an instant, AI consumes the vast reservoir of human intellectual history, depleting centuries of accumulated information.

This mechanical, formulaic processing model destroys the underlying logic that has nurtured human thought and development since ancient times. Human experience and cognition are reduced to physical or digital vectorized data, stripping away the organic complexities of reflection and growth. This shift has opened up a vast, boundless space for the degradation of thought and the emergence of an intellectually diminished society. Within this expanding void, the pathways of human understanding and the architecture of critical perception are being reshaped and reconstructed. The very possibilities of human cognition, the emergence of self-awareness and the formation of religion, ethics and belief systems are being fundamentally altered in this new landscape.

When information and knowledge no longer inspire imagination, willpower or emotional resonance, they become nothing more than piles of intellectual debris. Thus, the hollow ideology of AI, often described as 'non-ideological', represents an even more profound existential crisis for humanity – the virus infiltrates the central nervous system of human cognition. Its spread and influence, fuelled by corporate greed and unchecked capital, are virtually unstoppable. This marks a decisive turning point in human history, an event with consequences as profound as any mythological tale.

We often describe modern technologies as 'convenient', 'instant' and 'effortless', qualities once reserved for the realm of fantasy. Yet every meaningful, memorable human experience is rooted in struggle, perseverance and the complexity of life's challenges. This sense of exhilaration and fulfilment has now been replaced by effortless keystrokes, requiring neither strain nor effort.

The rise of AI is fundamentally altering our perception of space and time, and with it the ethical foundations of society, particularly our understanding of freedom. Concepts like effort, sacrifice, responsibility and duty, which have been the cornerstones of human growth and development, are disappearing. As these ancient values erode, so too does human dignity, individuality and personal rights.

Human beings are endowed by the heavens with a sense of moral existence and inherent rights, but these will ultimately disintegrate because the very mode of individual existence is being erased by AI's collective knowledge and informational structures. Humanity has finally created a tool that renders the existence of the individual self meaningless.

What people must recognize is that the true nature of the age of AI and intelligent machines is the Warring States period of intense competition between countries, driven by vast capital and vested interests. Human value is being replaced by the logic of profit, inevitably leading humanity towards a bewildering and savage new era.

The unification brought about by AI has accomplished what traditional censorship systems could never achieve: it has once again trivialized politically correct discourse, replacing humanity's capacity for critical thinking and dissent with conformity. The transformative power of heterodoxy and deviation within human thought is being systematically neutralized.

How Does Censorship Harm?

In a society where individual will and identity have been obliterated, whether under dictatorship, extreme capitalism or consumerism's monopolized version of the 'free world', existence becomes a mere fantasy. The unique attributes of individuals – their consciousness, principles, sense of boundaries, desire for exchange, potential for interaction and capacity for expression – are alienated, ultimately vanishing. What emerges from this void? It is a society that is numb, devoid of emotional depth, perception and creativity. It lacks insights, active thinking and the ability to question. It cannot discover meaningful questions or propose solutions. Human civilization becomes trapped in a state of anxious ignorance, marked by self-mockery and self-consolation. Such a society's numbness and arbitrariness stems from a pervasive, deeply ingrained mediocrity in its value system, and the complete devaluation and disappearance of individual values. No form of control – be it social, religious or otherwise – has ever produced a society so unconsciously detached.

At this point, censorship penetrates deeply into the fabric of existence, embedding itself into every individual's psyche. Technological censorship transcends ideologies, pushing self-censorship into the very core of life. This fundamental shift alters both societal and individual modes of existence. Life itself becomes hollow, reduced to bodies without spirits – mere living dead.

Censorship and the Shaping of Ideas

Here, I would like to quote a passage from an article written by my father in 1942, which became the catalyst for the Chinese Communist Party's early and intense censorship and ideological purges:

> I often hear people say: 'Certain individuals were displeased after reading a particular piece of work.' That, to me, is cause for great satisfaction –

> because it means the work has truly had an impact.
>
> . . .
>
> Writers ask for no privileges other than the freedom to write. One of the fundamental reasons they uphold democratic politics with their very lives is that democracy guarantees the independent spirit of artistic creation. Only when artistic creation is granted such freedom and independence can art play a role in advancing social reform.
>
> Ai Qing, *Understanding Writers and Respecting Writers*, March 1942

Looking back at this article, we can see that in its early years, when the Chinese Communist Party was still operating in the remote Yan'an region and at its most vulnerable, its censorship system was already severe – functioning much like an immune system that resists foreign invasion. Today, the censorship mechanisms prevalent in the 'free' world bear striking similarities to those of authoritarian regimes. It can be said that this is a collapse of human values and ethical systems.

At the core of human self-awareness and self-evaluation lie a set of ideals, beliefs and a sense of the intrinsic worth of the individual – these define our existence. When privacy disintegrates and modern society faces collapse, censorship and self-censorship are the first things to emerge.

In discussions of censorship, it is often perceived as no more than an act of elimination – a process of deleting or blocking an existing body of information, a form of filtration. But from Socrates in ancient Greece to the Chinese Warring States period, successive regimes and dynasties have consistently reshaped ideological narratives through a process of selection and reconstruction. Thus, censorship is not a passive act. It is something far more profound – an indispensable social mechanism tied to the very existence of rulers and those in power.

It is deeper than you might imagine. In the process of censorship, what the censors focus on is the reconstruction of both societal and individual cognition, aiming to reshape people's ideological frameworks. The very existence of censors is grounded in the pursuit of a clear, unified system of thought and consciousness. Their actions are deliberate and necessary, because within any system of censorship, there is always an active party – one that benefits from the suppression. Their goal is to eradicate any form of dissenting thought or questioning. This erasure can mean the literal disappearance of individuals – through imprisonment, exile or even death.

In modern societies, this disappearance renders thinkers and dissenters powerless, depriving them of both social recognition and self-evaluation, ultimately leading to what can be described as social death. Such phenomena and cases are far from rare.

When critical thinking is extinguished, what remains is an ideology tailored to serve the interests of the censors – an ideology that infiltrates every aspect of public life. It manifests in traditional media, print and television, in entertainment programmes, mainstream news and across social media platforms, from Hollywood to various online entertainment outlets. The publishing industry, the education sector and academia are not spared; they are all subject to both the pervasive influence of censorship and the subtle, underlying awareness of being censored.

Ideological control is as omnipresent as the air we breathe, because censorship has always been the primary tool for those in power to maintain their dominance.

Power, by its very nature, does not tolerate questions about its rationality or even its legitimacy. Thus, any doubts about the rationality or legality of power are the first to be targeted and eliminated through censorship. All platforms that shape public life and opinion – cultural institutions, museums, performing arts spaces and the publishing world – become the primary battlegrounds of censorship.

Censorship in Education

Censorship, both explicit and implicit, is particularly blatant in the field of education. In 2023 and 2024, some of America's most prestigious universities – Harvard, Columbia, MIT and the University of California – were entangled in events so bizarre they defied belief. Under pressure from their boards, university presidents were forced to step down. Students came under investigation by the FBI – some were arrested, charged and even deported. This was not an isolated occurrence, but part of a broader phenomenon that affects how young people think. In simplified terms, their social advancement and success are a kind of negotiated compromise with what they believe they must do – often at the cost of their ideals and principles. This compromise becomes the very precondition for a society's moral corruption.

These incidents, rooted in thought control and restrictions on freedom of expression, are merely the tip of the iceberg – the visible part floating above the surface. The larger, submerged portion is not only invisible to us, but has already been absorbed into the collective bloodstream of mainstream consciousness.

Power operates by the forced infusion of a certain ideology through education, mainstream media propaganda, consumption or the distortion and overheating of value systems. Why? This is the most important measure of its own existence: when its legitimacy is challenged, power has to fool the public's ability to think. Censorship is a basic precondition of power. Its popular discourse, through public media and education, and its underlying reality, the censorship of thought, are both geared to make it seem that the continuation of power is in the interests of the public, and of the stabilization or 'civilization' of society.

Social media platforms like X/Twitter and Facebook play equally astonishing roles in this ecosystem – engaging in both active and passive censorship under governmental influence, targeting information and ideas deemed undesirable. Mainstream media outlets like CNN are even more blatant, openly participating in such practices without pretence. At its core, censorship functions in fundamentally the same way under authoritarian regimes and in so-called free societies.

My Personal Experience of Censorship

In today's China, I have seen my articles deleted and censored, my exhibitions cancelled and even my name and works erased from exhibitions and

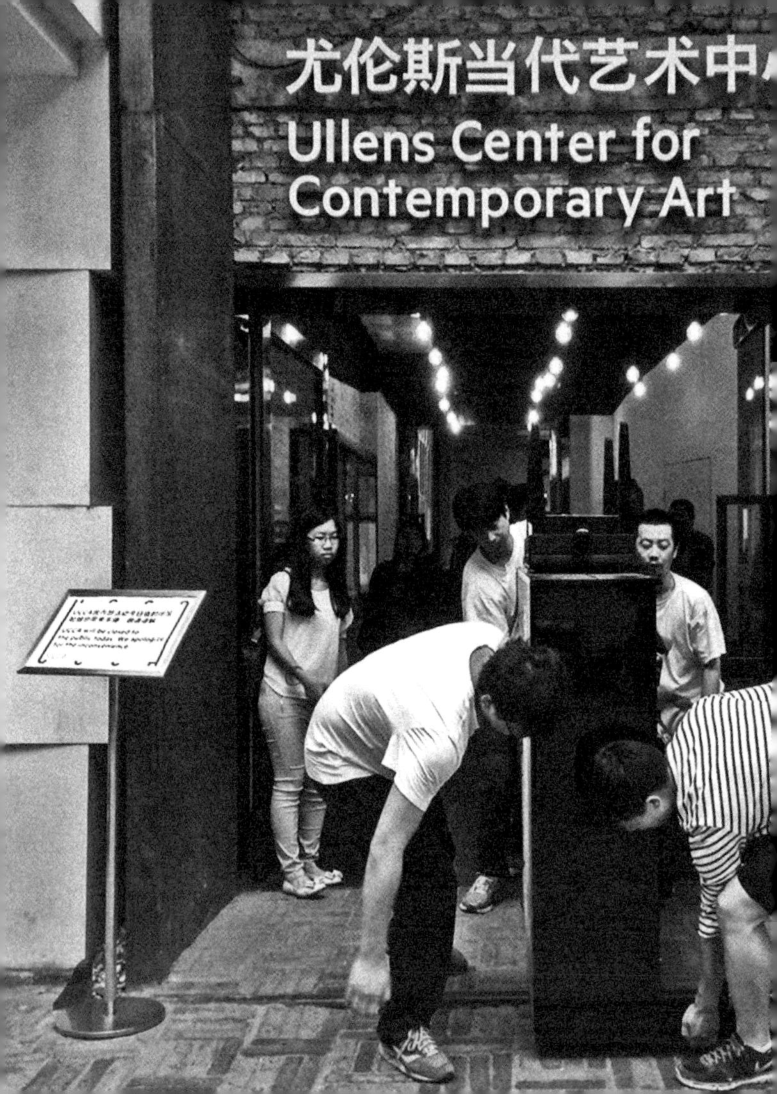
尤伦斯当代艺术中
Ullens Center for
Contemporary Art

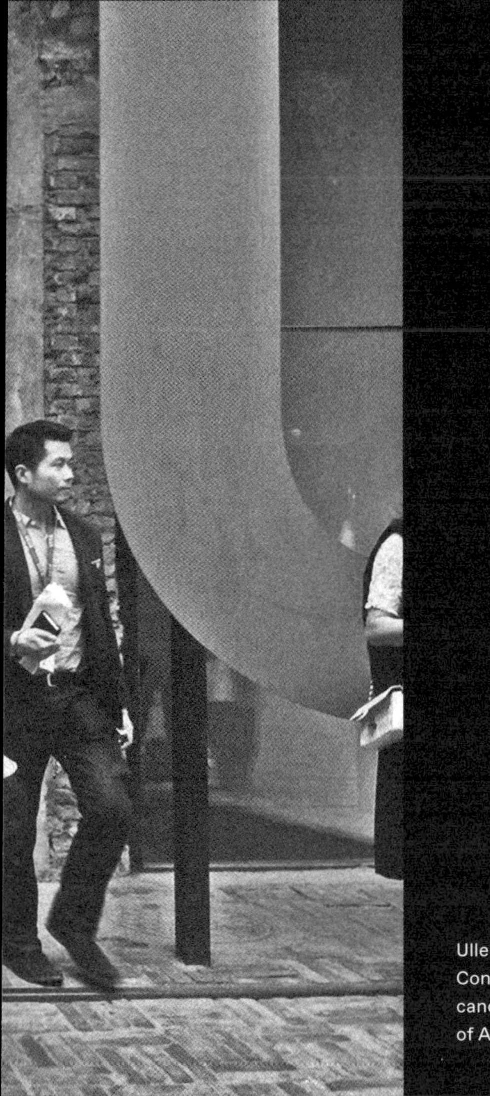

Ullens Center for
Contemporary Art (UCCA)
cancellation and removal
of Ai Weiwei's show, 2011

social media platforms. But this was not enough – not nearly enough.

The authorities go further, filling these voids with malicious attacks and distorted narratives, spreading lies to rewrite the public record. Authoritarian regimes despise empty spaces – they see absence as a form of protest, much like silence can be an act of defiance. They need to fill these gaps with loud noise and slander, contaminating spaces that once belonged to genuine voices. While this may seem absurd, the absurdity lies not only in the foolishness of their actions but also in the perverse logic that underpins their existence.

In history books published during these years, my name was replaced with someone else's and photos featuring me were blurred, pixellated like censored images from sex scenes.

In an art publication from London, my page, in English, was replaced – I suspect with the complicity of western editors – with another artist's work. Such details reveal the ruthless precision of censorship, a system that leaves no room for oversight. Even photos showing only my silhouette or my back are frequently subject to censorship.

After I was forced to leave China in 2015, I encountered a near-universal phenomenon: for almost every international museum exhibition, the corporate sponsors and foundations – once eager to support public art – withdrew their funding. The reason was always the same: I was labelled a politically sensitive figure in China, and they feared jeopardizing their business interests with the Chinese government.

At the National Museum of History in Mexico, my large-scale public artwork – the twelve zodiac sculptures titled *Circle of Animals/Zodiac Heads* – was forcibly removed from an ongoing exhibition at the direct request of the Chinese Embassy in Mexico. The demand was aggressive, and Mexico had no choice but to comply with this pressure.

This wasn't limited to museums. Major film festivals also rejected several of my films without clear explanations. Initially, these festivals expressed great enthusiasm, praising my films as 'moving' and 'unconventional'. But ultimately, I received the same standard rejection letter time and again.

These events may seem like distant, isolated incidents, but for an individual, they can be devastating. In another instance, a comment I made on social media resulted in the postponement and cancellation of exhibitions in Paris, London, Berlin and Boston. None of this surprises me. These experiences only reaffirm the necessity of free speech, which serves as the moral and ethical foundation of freedom of expression.

Those Who Control the Narrative Control the Future

Gaining absolute control over discourse through censorship is the most convenient and effective means of political domination. Freedom of speech represents the last line of defence against the collapse of individual consciousness or the collective awareness of a society. Censorship not only removes obstacles in the political environment for those in power, but also eradicates the voices of entire groups, generations or even multiple generations. It dismantles critical thinking, the capacity to distinguish between right and wrong, good and evil, ultimately forging a society devoid of consciousness, motivation, agency or judgment.

What we refer to as public consciousness, often termed social ethics, encompasses the moral standards of a society as a whole. Its formation originates from a society's educational system and the moral codes propagated by mainstream media. By controlling the completeness of information – offering only limited, curated data – societies inevitably shape perception. Such limitation and manipulation are nearly unavoidable, because our understanding of facts and the information we consume forms our conception of truth. It's akin to food processing, involving deliberate choices influenced by underlying ideological forces.

When such limited, distorted information is widely accepted, even becoming a dominant ideology, its harm far exceeds that of ignorance or mere lack of knowledge. Harmful information fosters blind conformity, and blind conformity is the breeding ground for violence – precisely the optimal condition that censors seek to achieve.

In western societies, these censors are often the forces of large capital interests, driven by the immense profits and temptations generated by ruthless competition for survival. By purging minds of authentic information and replacing it with chaotic, distorted narratives, combined with the seductive comforts of material wealth, complacency and manipulated education and public discourse, people's growth, values, friendships and life paths are subtly controlled. Individuals seek validation from the group, conforming to collective norms to attain a sense of belonging and security. Moral coercion becomes an invisible yet inescapable force shaping one's sense of existence. The success of these factors is precisely why censorship persists.

Censorship undoubtedly provides a flawed, distorted framework for judgment, creating blind spots and obstacles in a society's ability to self-correct and recognize its own biases. It triggers collective conformity, eroding the capacity for independent decision-making and reducing people to powerless bystanders or unwitting enforcers – mere sheep following the herd. By weakening individual judgment, censorship eliminates personal agency, dismantles moral standards for discerning right from wrong and extinguishes the possibility of transparency and fairness.

Every society – whether authoritarian or part of the so-called free West – employs different forms of indoctrination to guide behaviour, shaping people's cognition, capacity for action and modes of thinking. Simultaneously, it numbs the perception of reality, leaving public consciousness in a paralysed state. In this numbness, people abandon their judgment, and eventually it disappears altogether. The capacity for independent thought fades, and a personal view on history and reality disappears, as does the capacity to question. That's how censorship, to a large extent, reshapes how social development is interpreted. It not only redefines self-awareness and historical understanding but also alters people's judgment and expectations for the future.

In today's highly polarized political landscape, characterized by division and confrontation, censorship is increasingly becoming a kind of trademark, allowing it once again to display the starkest characteristics of power politics, regardless of whether we examine the contemporary U.S. political climate or major tech companies' prominent online speech platforms. Censorship reveals itself even more vividly as an instrument of power politics precisely because these entities must coexist, side by side. In their attempts to distort public discourse, forces of power – be they political, ideological or financial – resort to increasingly overt and undisguised censorship measures. The ultimate objective behind these actions is, to a significant extent, to exert control over public opinion.

Under this kind of control, when information is censored, cancelled, altered or distorted, a significant gap is inevitably left behind – a void typically filled by what we call 'fake news'. Regimes, institutions or organizations that engage in censorship simultaneously produce fake news and misinformation as their fundamental practice. If they succeed in erasing truthful and reliable information, their actions naturally require, support or even encourage them to fill the resulting void in public discourse with false narratives. This creates a double-bind situation: by restricting and censoring truth, these entities also endorse and promote untruth or misinformation. In most cases, they themselves become the propagators and supporters of fake information. A society based on this mechanism faces a clear prospect: information, a critical pillar of society – both ethically and in terms of social progress – loses its essential function. The general public experiences a consequent profound lack of confidence and a sense of confusion, uncertain about where to find reliable information. Eventually, they may even abandon the pursuit of truth altogether. This, precisely, is the most crucial strategy of an authoritarian state.

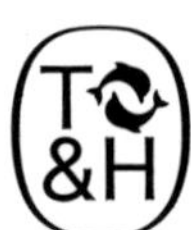
T&H

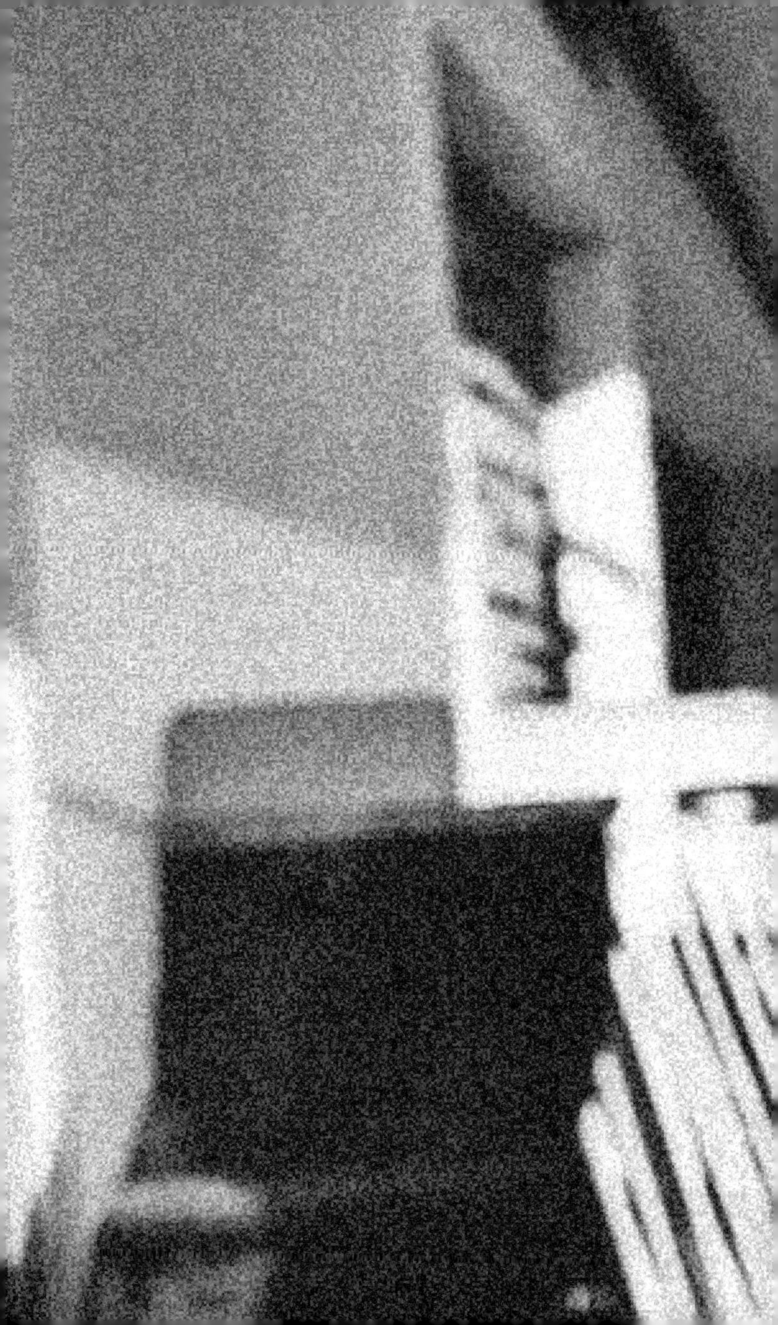

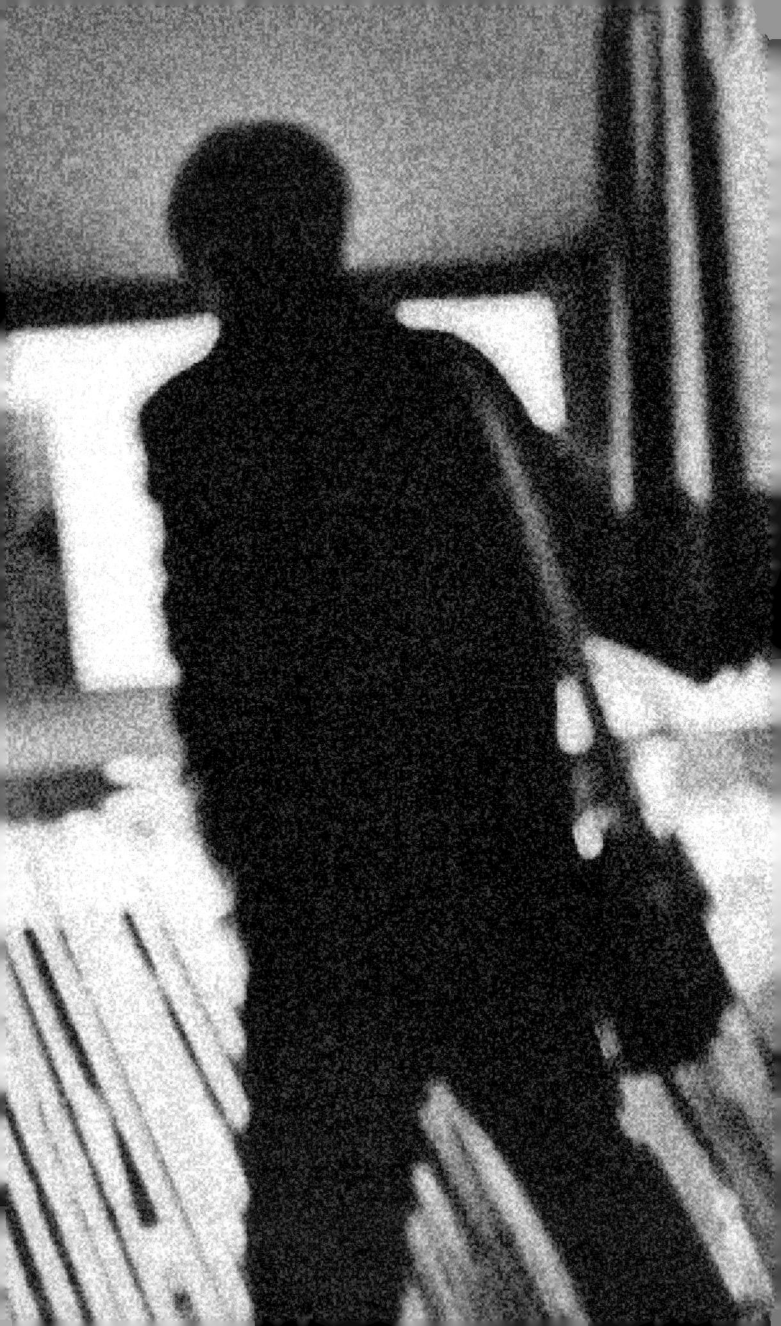